The Teaching of Judo
An Instructor's Handbook

Mark E. Roosa

The Teaching of Judo: An Instructor's Handbook

Published by Wheatmark®
1760 East River Road, Suite 145, Tucson, Arizona 85718 USA
www.wheatmark.com

ISBN: 978-1-62787-320-8 (paperback)
ISBN: 978-1-62787-321-5 (ebook)
LCCN: 2015911958

Cover design and artwork by Shannon Barteau.

Author's Note

The ideas and opinions in this book are strictly my own and have been derived from my years as a judo instructor and professional educator. Teaching anything is a monumental responsibility when you consider how it can affect people's lives. This book does not include in-depth studies of human behavior or teaching styles. Rather, it is designed to be a quick reference guide to give beginning instructors a place to start and to help them avoid certain common pitfalls in running a dojo. It might also be useful to experienced instructors who want to strengthen or better organize their programs. Parents, too, might find the book useful when searching for a competent instructor for their children. The reader should keep in mind that successful judo instruction is a complicated integration of several factors covered in this book. There are many avenues to success, and my ideas and opinions certainly cannot cover them all. You have my sincere wishes for success. Judo needs great teachers.

Table of Contents

Foreword

I was honored to be asked first to read through Mark Roosa's book entitled *The Teaching of Judo*, and then to write his foreword. I find it refreshing to see a Judo textbook that actually addresses the processes used to share techniques, philosophies, and skills with students, rather than solely covering the presentation of a limited set of tachiwaza and newaza techniques. This novel perspective reflects Mark's passion as an educator as well as his resilience as a judoka.

A professional educator myself, I was finding myself exclaiming "Hear, hear!" to the style and presentation of each chapter. For example, it was exciting to see a Judo textbook finally addressing children with special needs as an instructional focus group. Having had children with disabilities both in my classroom and in our dojo for nearly three decades, I found his advice insightful and refreshing.

I have refereed many of Mark's students over the years. He does a phenomenal job developing quality judoka who are not only good technicians, but good people. They also have developed a sense of strategy in their competition that reflects a deep understanding of the sport.

I highly recommend this book for those who are looking for a fresh perspective of the process of sharing their judo knowledge with others.

Janet Yoshie Ashida Johnson
Rokudan, IJF A Referee

Introduction

Over the nearly fifty years that I have been involved in judo as a competitor, coach, referee, and instructor, I have been fortunate enough to observe and practice with some of the finest judoka and judo instructors in the world. Each one had a special talent or message to offer. Most judo books are technical manuals for performing the many variations of techniques in judo. The purpose of this book, however, is to provide a manual of instruction for black-belt judoka who decide to open dojos (schools). In addition, it may be useful to someone seeking a judo school that offers safe and sensible quality instruction.

Properly teaching judo is critical for our art/sport to survive and flourish. I believe that the teachings of Dr. Jigoro Kano, the founder of judo, have expanded beyond his wildest dream. In many ways I think he would be pleased, especially because judo is now the second most popular sport in the world. On the other hand, I believe he would be disappointed in how the focus of judo has changed. Since the inclusion of judo in the Olympic Games in 1964, the focus of judo has shifted increasingly toward winning world medals and away from developing quality human beings and superb technicians. As a result, the almighty dollar has become the driving force behind judo. Each year it seems the cost of judo escalates so that the expense of participating discourages more prospective students. The need for quality grassroots instructors is more important than ever before. Nearly all high-level competitors in judo got their starts in local grassroots judo programs before advancing to high-level training somewhere else.

At the time of this writing (2014), teaching judo has become quite complex for anyone running a dojo. There is so much to know and think about that a reference manual for the day-to-day operation should prove invaluable to many instructors, especially for those just starting out. The focus of this book is the instruction of fundamental judo concepts to students interested in recreational judo or competitive judo up to about the shodan or nidan level. If your desire is to only train world-class judoka, this book is probably not for you.

Over the years, I have often received unusual compliments about my instruction—for example, that my students had much better technique and were more successful in shiai (tournaments) than would be expected from an instructor with relatively little competitive experience. Those people making these comments did not realize that my gift is not that of competitive athleticism but rather being able to teach people how to do things correctly. My strength has always been the ability to spot flaws in technique and correct them in a coherent manner.

My credentials for this book go beyond my godan rank. I have thirty-five years of experience teaching physics, earth science, and math to go along with my three education degrees. In addition, I have also refereed judo on the national and international level for over twenty years, and my club has placed a few people on the national level, even though it is not the focus of my instruction. Having been in numerous dojos over the past forty-five years, I have been both impressed and appalled at some of the teaching techniques that I have observed. They range from absolutely brilliant to downright dangerous. Hopefully this book will help instructors teach judo more effectively and more safely.

Acknowledgments

I would like to thank a host of people for their input into my judo education and their often unwitting participation in the development of this book. I owe much to my experiences with these judoka, including a few whose names I have regrettably forgotten. Sincere thanks to the following:

Mr. N. Adams, Dr. S Ashida, Mr. J. Bassano, Mr. J. Bregman, Mr. P. Capra, Mr. R. Cellato, Mr. R. Court, Mr. T. Dalton, Mr. D. Draeger, Mr. M. Eguchi, Mr. R. Fountain, Mr. K. Freeman, Ms. K. Fukuda, Mr. T. Grisanti, Mr. H. S. Han, Mr. J. Hrbek, Mr. R. Hugh, Mr. I. Inokuma, Mr. K. Inoue, Ms. J. Johnson, Mr. and Mrs. R. Kanokogi, Mr. S. Kelly, Mr. T. Kidachi, Mr. N. Kudo, Mr. P Legros, Mr. W. Martin, Mr. L. McCloskey, Mr. T. Merck, Mr. N. Ogasawara, Mr. S. Oishi, Mr. H. Omichi, Mr. A. Parisi, Mr. R. Reyes, Mr. M. Roper, Mr. W. Scribner, Mr. T. Sengoku, Ms. K. Shiina, Mr. G. Spadin, Mr. M. Swain, Mr. K. Takata, Mr. C. Wall, Mr. K. Watanabe, Mr. C. Worthen, and Mr. Y. Yonezuka.

I also owe thanks to all the members of Hudson Judo Yudanshakai and Ulster Budokai Inc. Thanks to my wife and family for encouraging me to write down what I have learned. I am also indebted to my proofreaders, Tom Merck, Bill Scribner, Zach Baum, Wayne Olson, Janet Johnson, and especially Ezra Waltermaurer, who doubled as my photographer.

Chapter 1

Philosophy of Teaching

If you are going to teach any subject, you owe it to your students to do the best job that you can. After all, your students' successes, failures, and even their safety depend to a large degree on what you teach and how you instruct them. It is wise to ask yourself what your philosophy of teaching is or, more simply, why you are doing this. For example, my philosophy of teaching is to teach people by giving them the information and tools to help them make informed, intelligent decisions. This statement may not sound much like a judo instruction philosophy, but it works for me.

Once you have a teaching philosophy, you can apply it to your methods of instruction. It often helps clarify whether you are teaching something because you particularly like it or because it will help your students progress. I might add at this time that I believe judo to be a lifelong study and that we are all students. I have yet to spend a year in judo where I didn't learn something new. Keep in mind that judo was designed as an educational system suitable for public and private schools. In principle, judo encompasses physical training, mental training, and moral issues such as sportsmanship and citizenship. The goals and lessons of judo instruction include the development of mind and body, respect for others, discipline, strategy, hygiene, appreciation of other cultures, and the development of other higher moral values. Your philosophy of teaching will hopefully help you clarify your role and your goals in teaching judo. In my philosophy, I have come to realize that my role is to serve as a conduit to the proper execution of judo technique and knowledge. My goal is to develop quality judo technicians and students who represent judo in a positive and respectful manner.

Dr. Kano himself stressed the importance of teaching when he said, "Nothing is of greater importance than education; the teachings of one virtuous man can reach many, and that which has been learned by one generation can be passed on to a hundred."

Chapter 2

The Core Curriculum

Dr. Kano provided us with an invaluable tool when he gave us the gokyo no waza. This outline of throwing techniques is a living, flexible guide to instruction. The concept of a core curriculum focuses on the very basic components of instruction and learning required to build a foundation for advanced learning. In judo, this core encompasses falling, etiquette, throws, pins, chokes, armlocks, grips, movement, defense, escapes, and more. In many dojos, I've observed the instruction centered on the instructor's likes and dislikes, and especially his or her favorite technique, instead of a core curriculum of judo. I once observed a dojo where ukemi (falling) was severely neglected and poorly taught. Imagine my surprise when I discovered that this particular dojo had a high dropout rate due to injuries.

Every instructor will have some variation in his or her basic curriculum. However, the neglect of any basic component may lead to slow or poor development, or worse yet, to injuries. I believe any study of introductory judo should cover the following brief summary of basics, whether the focus is on competition or simply recreation. This core curriculum should cover from one to three years of practice, depending on the age and abilities of students and the frequency and length of practices. There are many excellent books and videos about technical instruction. I have used many in writing this book and listed them in the bibliography. In my own dojo, we keep copies of *Kodokan Judo*, by Jigoro Kano, and *Textbook of Judo*, by Nagayasu Ogasawara, which are available as quick references for students and instructors alike.

Core Curriculum

I) Etiquette: The proper methods of bowing, sitting, and standing and the correct procedure for getting up and down. Respect for elders and ranking judoka.

II) Hygiene: Clean body, clean gi, and fingernails and toenails trimmed. Dojo is clean.

III) History of Judo: Dr. Kano, brief chronology, famous judoka (T. Roosevelt, Putin, etc.). US judo history (or native country if other than United States).

IV) Principles of maximum efficiency and mutual welfare and benefit (seiryoku-zen'yo and jita-kyoei). Methods of breaking balance (happo no kuzushi).

V) Ukemi: Front, back, and side falls. Zenpo kaiten (rollouts), front and rear.

VI) Ne waza: Groundwork; tori on top and on back.
  A. Turnovers: Uke on all fours, hands and knees, and tori on top. Also tori on back with uke between tori's legs.
  B. Osaekomi: Pins or holds.
  C. Shime waza: Choking techniques (age appropriate).
  D. Kansetsu waza: Joint lock techniques (rank appropriate).
  E. Escapes from moves A through D.
  F. Transitions from moves A through D.

VII) Nage waza: Throwing techniques.
  A. Te waza: Hand techniques.
  B. Koshi waza: Hip techniques.

    C. Ashi waza: Foot and leg techniques.
    D. Sutemi waza: Sacrifice techniques (at sankyu or nikyu level).
    E. Defense: Blocks and counters.
    F. Combinations (appropriate for rank and skill level).
    G. Gripping.
    H. Movement and set up for throws (timing).

This core curriculum will be expanded in a later chapter that includes suggestions for teaching it. All techniques are appropriate based on age, rank, and physical ability. This outline gives the instructor both group and individual plans of instruction. Developing both left- and right-side techniques, starting in the first six months of instruction, is also important.

Chapter 3

Where Do We Start?

Good judo instruction starts outside the class setting. First, an adequate practice area, a minimum of three hundred square feet is needed, and quality mats are essential. Wrestling mats on concrete or a gym floor are not adequate and will lead to needless injuries. There are many good ideas for safe mat areas. Visiting a few dojos will provide plenty of information to solve the problem.

An initial expense of $10,000 is not unusual, but with a little ingenuity and teamwork, a group can get started for much less. Some YMCAs, schools, and community organizations are willing to at least partially sponsor judo programs. The information found in an excellent book by Michel Brousse and David Matsumoto, *Judo: a Sport and a Way of Life*, especially chapter 7 on the qualities and benefits of judo, can often convince people who are ignorant of judo values to try a judo program in their communities.

If you are not going to be a professional instructor, set up a reasonable fee schedule to cover dojo expenses. Make sure to obtain insurance for the dojo (especially in the United States). Liability and accident insurance are available through USA Judo, USJF, and USJA. If you are concerned about lawsuits (and you should be), consider incorporation as a small business to add an extra layer of legal protection for your personal property. Caution students without health insurance that the deductible on medical insurance can be very high. Also, note that the insurance is not valid unless everyone on the mat is insured. Many instructors carry a liability rider on their personal homeowner's insurance as well.

Professional instructors, of course, have to be concerned with earning a living, and I admittedly have no experience with this type of venture. I can only assume that the student rates would be considerably higher and that a greater number of students may be required.

Make sure to keep an attendance roster for each class. Having a written record of who was or was not in class is not only valuable in evaluating student progress for ranking purposes, but can also be critical in matters concerning injury insurance claims or legal situations.

Now structure your class pattern. Write it down and keep a copy in your attendance book. Parents love to see an organized instructor. Listed below is the basic class structure that I have followed for years. Keep in mind that it is flexible and does not have to be used for every class.

Structure for a 1.5- to 2-Hour Class

I) Bow-in and warm-ups, including ukemi: fifteen to twenty minutes. Students come to class to practice judo, not to do calisthenics. Most of the warm-ups should be stretching or judo-related exercises to prevent muscle strains. Conditioning is another topic.

II) Ne waza: twenty-five to forty minutes. I usually allow ten minutes for instruction.

III) Uchikomi and nage waza instruction: twenty-five to forty minutes. I allow ten minutes for instruction.

IV) Randori: twenty-five to forty minutes.

V) Cool-down and bow-out: five minutes.

Total: 95 to 145 minutes.

Of course, these times can be modified according to what is planned for each lesson. For example, some nights we might have forty minutes of ne waza and sixty minutes of randori, decreasing the other three areas accordingly. The experience level of your students and the number of assistants that you have can greatly affect the amount of time needed for each section of the lesson.

It is essential to get your students into a routine for the structure of class. Students feel more comfortable when they know what to expect next in the routine. Even so, that certainly does not mean that you shouldn't change that routine occasionally to prevent monotony from developing.

Chapter 4

Becoming a Competent Instructor (I'm a Plumber, not a Teacher)

You do not have to be a trained educator to be a competent judo instructor. A little common sense, a good plan, and attention to detail will go a long way. Most of us know great judo competitors who are not great at teaching, or we know the reverse, mediocre competitors who consistently turn out quality students. While it's nice to get the best of both worlds, it isn't always possible. The following are some hints on being a quality teacher. Sample basic lesson plans follow.

Quality teachers in any field have certain attributes in common:

1) Honesty
2) Fairness
3) Work ethic—don't ask students to do things you wouldn't do yourself
4) Humility
5) Responsibility—doing the best job you are capable of
6) Discipline—prompt, prepared, consistent, respectful
7) Adaptability—can adjust when things don't go as planned

8) Understanding of their subject (how to establish a solid foundation)
9) Open-minded—willing to entertain different ideas

How do you learn to teach? Well, there's a lot of trial and error, but a few guidelines make learning to teach easier. Use what works, and discard what does not work.

1) Prepare what you intend to teach ahead of time. Spur-of-the-moment instruction is seldom as effective.
2) Imitate the best. If you see something great, steal it and incorporate it.
3) Do not teach what you do not fully understand. Defer to an expert when possible. As Clint Eastwood said in one of his movies, "A man has to know his limitations."
4) Understand student limitations. For example, the average person has an attention span of approximately twenty minutes. After that, you've lost them.
5) Be flexible. Keep in mind that, as with most things in life, there is more than one way to do something well. Good variations of techniques abound in judo. Your way may not be the best.
6) Don't teach too much. It is far easier to learn one technique in a lesson than it is to learn three moves and their variations. Refer to number four.
7) Teach, practice, refine, and repeat often. Guided repetition is essential to developing good technique.
8) Involve your students in setting goals. Let them know your goals for them and ask them their goals. Attempt to make yours and theirs match. Short-term goals work best. I recently had a teenage student announce a goal to me. He said that he was sick of his ippon seoinage not working well and that he was going to do three hundred fit-ins (uchikomi) each week for the next six months. What could I do but agree?

Options to Make the Job Easier

Involve parents and the community. Parents normally want to share their children's progress and often join judo to more closely share the experience. Parents can be recruited to help with repairs, do fund-raising, carpool students to practice and tournaments, and many other things. In the community, there are many opportunities to educate people about judo and about your dojo in particular. Demonstrations can bring in new students, advertise your program, and occasionally lead to expanded programs or outside financial support for your students. Our dojo has not only gained financial support for competitors but also expanded our program to include special needs classes for autistic children though the community autism society.

Use social media to make people aware of what your program has to offer and to advertise upcoming events or student performance. These days, every dojo should have its own website.

Share the responsibility by forming a dojo instruction team. For example, if you have a student who has exceptional falling skills, put him or her in charge of teaching beginners their basic ukemi. The main thing is to make sure that your team is teaching the same things to all students. Other sources of help are obvious. Read, watch quality video, and go to clinics with the best technicians in your area. Record these clinics on video if it's allowed (a good parent job), take notes, and remember to ask questions.

Instructor Responsibilities

1) Keep learning—it's a lifelong journey.
2) Keep an open mind. There are many roads to success.
3) Be a positive role model.
4) Share ideas and seek feedback. Enhance the learning process.
5) Be humble.
6) Use positive reinforcement. Instead of saying, "That's wrong," try saying, "Let's make this throw a little stronger."

7) Focus part of your time on character development. Developing a black belt who acts like an arrogant idiot is not a success story.

8) Teach to enhance the growth of judo. Partner with other clubs and share information.

9) Student safety is a priority, both in practice and tournament.

The Lesson Plan

A good lesson plan in a dojo presents a challenge because each class can have a different student population. The class can vary in size and student skill level. A prepared instructor always has an alternate plan, usually an old favorite, for the times when class attendance does not match the lesson plan. Written lesson plans are recommended. They make great references, keep you on track, and can always be used again.

Lesson Plan Format

A. Statement of objective—clear purpose with any variations. Keep it simple.

B. Input. How you are going to teach. Start simple and work toward complex.

C. Modeling should be clear and correct. Show from different angles.

D. Check for understanding. This may require further input.

E. Guided practice.

F. Closure—summary feedback or questions from students.

G. Independent practice.

Remember that this format should be a flexible model and may not contain each component. I often sequence three or four lessons together on the same technique, always working from simple to complex. This allows for consistent repetition and review as well as for an extension of the technique into situations, combinations, counters, or possible variations. Also keep in mind that a lesson plan is a living document and should be revised and improved periodically. The following are two simple lesson plans that I have used for many years.

Lesson Plan for Basic Osoto gari (see photos)

    A. Statement of Objective: Teach osoto gari on its basic level. Stress the proper use of hands and precise foot position.

    B. Input: Right-side osoto. From standard grip, tori positions the center of his or her chest in line with uke's right shoulder. Left foot enters deep and parallel to uke's right foot. Tori's left hand presses uke's right arm out and back to open shoulder. Right hand lifts uke's collar under the chin, keeping the elbow down under the hand (posting) and pressing backward. Making shoulder-to-shoulder contact, tori brings right leg through and past uke's right leg, keeping toes pointed down and knee slightly bent. Tori's right leg then reaps through from his or her hip, making calf-to-calf contact and executing the throw. Tori never places weight on reaping leg or places it on the mat during the execution of the throw. Osoto gari works best when uke steps forward on his or her right leg (timing).

osoto 1

osoto 2

osoto 3

osoto 4

C. Modeling: Demonstrate the throw, rotating ninety degrees each time. Do it in slow motion, emphasizing hands, feet, and contact; then do it again, quickly.

D. Check for Understanding: Ask questions.

E. Guided Practice: Uchikomi—two sets of twenty changing partners each set. Follow each set with five throws.

osoto 5

F. Closure: Reemphasize key points of kuzushi and entry. Give feedback. Have students demonstrate.

G. Independent Practice: A few minutes of free uchikomi, possibly on the move with experienced students.

My next two lesson plans are about setting the position for osoto gari and then using a left fake to set up osoto gari (similar to a left sasae tsuri komi ashi attempt). Fakes and combinations are for students who have more experience and reasonably good form developed.

Lesson Plan for Basic Okuri Eri Jime (see photos)

A. Statement of Objective: Teach okuri eri jime on its basic level. Stress proper hand position and leg control.

B. Input: Left-hand okuri eri jime. Uke is sitting, and tori is behind, kneeling on his or her right knee. With the right hand, tori reaches under uke's right armpit and grasps the right lapel, gripping it firmly and pulling it straight down to make the collar stiff and straight. Inserting the thumb of his left hand inside the straightened collar, tori slides thumb up as far as it will go and grasps the collar firmly, being careful to only hold as much collar as is necessary for a good grip. (Note: Tori's left index finger should be behind uke's right ear). Tori then releases his or her grip with the right hand, reaches across to the left lapel, and grips it firmly near the lower pectoral region of uke's chest. Keeping his or her head and chest close to uke's neck and back respectively, tori pulls the collar around and back with his or her left hand, keeping the heel of the hand in contact with uke's upper chest. (There should be contact between tori's chest and uke's back).

okuri 1

okuri 2

Tori simultaneously pulls uke's left collar straight down toward uke's hip with his or her right hand until uke signals submission. During the application, tori should press his or her left knee firmly against uke's left side to prevent uke from defending by rotating to the left.

okuri 3

C. Modeling: Demonstrate by facing students and then again facing ninety degrees to the left and right sides, illustrating the hand and leg positions. Emphasize using position and control instead of brute force.

D. Check for Understanding: Answer any questions.

E. Guided Practice: Students pair up, preferably with a novice and a more advanced student in each pair. Check each pair for the correct form. CAUTION: When teaching beginners, students may pass out if the technique is executed properly. Be prepared to revive them if needed and encourage them to submit before they pass out.

F. Closure: Reemphasize hand position and hand movement. Give feedback. Have several pairs demonstrate.

G. Independent Practice: Students regroup with different partners and now practice both the left- and right-side versions.

The follow-up lesson, which can be done at this time, is to teach the same choke with tori seated with his or her legs hooked around uke's legs from the rear, learning leg control to prevent uke from escaping.

Keep in mind that lesson plans are living documents and should be reviewed or changed to meet the needs of you and your students as you teach the core curriculum. Over the years, you will accumulate numerous lesson plans that will fall into categories called units. In these units will be sets of sequential lessons starting with simple techniques and leading into more complex versions and combinations. In my teaching experience, I have developed about one hundred separate lesson plans that I use on a regular basis.

Becoming a competent teacher, like many worthwhile talents, is a process where you become better by doing. You may not be an overnight success, but eventually you will learn what works and what doesn't. Observe as many judo instructors as possible and recall what characteristics impressed you of your own teachers in all phases of life. It can also be useful to recall the traits of teachers that you did not like. Were they boring, sarcastic, unprepared, confusing, or limited in their knowledge?

Keep in mind that there are many different teaching styles, and no one style is necessarily better than another. I have been told that my style is somewhat Socratic because I engage students in discussing and evaluating what is taught. There are numerous books on teaching styles if you are interested. The main thing, I believe, is to develop a style that fosters interest and opens doors for questions and improvement in what you teach. Avoid long lectures and keep your students actively practicing what is taught. Keep them on task. When you notice students straying from what you taught, it's time to move on to another variation or a different part of the lesson. Keep in mind that student attention span is not endless and that competent teachers know when their students have reached their limits.

Chapter 5

Etiquette, Discipline, and Rank

The question of whether to teach traditional Japanese dojo etiquette has been debated now for about the last twenty-five years. Traditionalists like me think this is common sense because it's the way we were trained. So I asked myself what the benefits are for taking the time to teach the etiquette. I also polled the opposing viewpoint. Those who were opposed had two arguments. First, that this is the United States and not Japan. Second, they felt that their students "just don't get it."

I have seen four dojos in the past ten years that have no bowing procedure before and after class and no bowing between students as they partner up. I'd like to tell you that their judo was weak and sloppy, but three of the four clubs had very solid judo, and the fourth was good with poor ukemi, which is another issue. My question was, "Do you (the instructor) embrace all of judo or just those parts that appeal to you?" The answer invariably went back to the aforementioned arguments.

The value of etiquette in the dojo to me is enforcing respect and discipline. When students understand that bowing is similar to shaking hands or a peck on the cheek in some European countries and that bowing has no religious significance, they are much more open to the concept. Second, the etiquette enhances the appreciation of other cultures. I always tell my students how baseball in Japan uses American terminology out of respect for the sport and our culture. I believe it is only fitting to reciprocate. The choice, of course, is yours.

Discipline in the dojo is often a controversial subject. When is it discipline and when is it abuse, either physical or verbal? Over the years, some of the things I've observed instructors doing to their students defy logic and sanity. Things like slapping them or calling them stupid when they lose, spitting in their faces, or kicking them when they are lying down. Fortunately, these incidents were rare. Any time you administer discipline in anger, you run the risk of being abusive. Discipline that degrades the person is normally nonproductive and abusive as well.

Most discipline in judo is about respect or safety. Judo discipline may be physically harsh at times as well as embarrassing. However, if the student knows that he or she is being disciplined for the behavior and that the behavior is disrespectful to judo or dangerous to someone in the dojo, the chances are high that a productive lesson will be learned. I've found that not being allowed to practice is an effective disciplinary tactic, especially for children. The best discipline is based on a student's respect for the instructor. Set reasonable guidelines, inform students of those guidelines, and be fair and consistent. Use humor where possible. Avoid disciplinary action when you are not in control of your temper, and be sure that your discipline is the same for all students.

It is a sad fact that occasionally a student does not embrace your philosophy of judo. This student may enjoy hurting his fellow judoka or refuse to change his or her arrogant, disrespectful behavior. Situations like these can only disrupt the harmony and educational climate of the dojo. If all attempts to correct the attitude and behavior fail, your only recourse is to remove that particular student (or students) from your dojo. In the long term, your dojo will be better off, and teaching class will be fun again.

Patience is a great virtue for an instructor. Not everyone gets it the first time. We all feel frustrated when we have difficulty understanding a concept or idea. Worse yet, we often get angry when we fail to perform up to expectations. As with most technical activities, time and repetition get the job done eventually. I like to remind my students and myself what the great Yogi Berra said, "Ninety percent of the game is half mental."

A gratifying part of being a judo instructor is watching students advance in rank. I still remember how excited I was when my first two students passed their black-belt requirements. We all know that there is a great disparity in the quality of rank from club to club, state to state, and country to country. Relax—it's not all bad.

In the grand scheme of judo, it usually evens out along the path of advancement. The main concern for an instructor is to choose fair and equitable requirements for all ranks, with provisions for age, physical disability, time in grade, and other factors. The ranking organizations have worked out reasonable requirements and have made them easily accessible. Rank is a reward for diligence, increased technical ability, contribution to judo, competitive achievement, and representing judo favorably outside the dojo. Requirements that are too tough discourage students. Requirements that are too easy make high rank appear cheap and insignificant.

Judo is a combative and competitive activity. Judoka who are not good competitors should take longer to advance and be required to have more knowledge, such as kata. Remember that judo has its roots in jujutsu and is in essence a martial art toned down to make it safe for everyone. Dan ranks in judo should exhibit some degree of skillful application in their judo. We cannot all be tenth dans. Often it is easier to evaluate and award rank when groups of students from a variety of clubs are brought together to demonstrate their skills.

Chapter 6

The Principle of Ju

In 1882 Dr. Kano created judo from jujutsu, an activity designed to train an individual both mentally and physically as well as to provide moral training to hopefully benefit society. Since that time, judo has evolved into a multifaceted international sport/art.

One facet of judo has developed into a dynamic, highly competitive sport. The power and stamina of these competitive athletes led many older judoka to wonder if they've lost touch with the basic principles of judo. In modern judo, so much emphasis is on strength and endurance, frequently before strong technical development. Purists cringe at a win by brute strength, while some coaches often appear happy just to achieve a victory. The modern national and international competitor is an amazing combination of strength, speed, endurance, strategy, aggressiveness, and sometimes technique too. The "old" judoka were often boring to watch as matches could last twenty minutes and were chess matches won by the first judoka to capitalize on an opponent's mistake.

Modern judo is often boring because of the emphasis on gripping and creative stalling once a judoka is ahead in a match. Penalties abound these days to deter negative judo but also create scenarios where Olympic titles are decided by shido instead of ippon. These rule changes have been well intended, trying to make a judo competition more exciting to watch by eliminating stalling, false attacks, and defensive escape tactics. Unfortunately, the refereeing is often inconsistent and appears to change sometimes at the whim of those in power on the international level.

However, like the proverbial beacon in the night, once every few years, a judoka appears with what appears to the uneducated to be a mystical ability. These judoka have an uncanny ability to score ippon with spectacular throws and devastating chokes, pins, and armlocks. Every judo enthusiast knows their names and techniques. Judoka like Y. Yamashita, T. Koga, U. Quellmalz, A. Geesink, N. Sato, I. Berghmans, K-Y Jeon, M. C. Restoux, I. Okano, R. Tani (Tamura), K. Inoue, and N. Adams, just to name a few (apologies to the many I've omitted), are admired and emulated throughout the judo world.

Of course, they are famous because they have won one or more major championships and have done it with style, often making it look easy! What do all these outstanding technicians have in common? Many things, I'm sure, but knowledgeable observers see that it's obvious that they understand the principle of ju or "gentleness."

Loosely translated, ju is the "giving way" to the strength of one's opponent and then using that strength to help defeat him or her. One of my old practice partners used to say that you would try to get the guy to throw himself to make it look like you knew what you were doing. For many judoka, ju is an elusive magic that all strive to master but few ever fully achieve. A judoka with one or two winning techniques is usually viewed as an accomplished judoka. However, many of the great technicians that I have been privileged to observe and practice with had the uncanny ability to take advantage of nearly every movement their opponents made and effortlessly turn it into ippon. As a young judoka, I was determined to learn the magic and emulated these judoka. The harder I tried, the worse my judo seemed to work.

The secret was finally revealed to me at a clinic in Hawaii in 1978. A hachidan from Japan, Professor Kudo, gave a clinic to all the instructors at the tournament. Between stepping off the mat to smoke and stepping back on the mat to effortlessly throw his uke, he stressed the importance of teaching our students to spend most of their randori time playing "loose," with the use of strength discouraged.

It turned my personal judo around (better late than never), and I began to develop higher-quality judo students. However, loosening up in practice is not that easy. A judoka who practices this way usually gets thrown more often, especially in the beginning. The ego must be put aside, and the person must realize that being thrown in practice can actually be productive in correcting mistakes in one's posture or movement. Judoka who learn to relax their strength until the proper moment learn to feel their opponents' movements and more consistently apply techniques at the most opportune times.

In his book *Classical Judo*, Don Draeger explains the misconceptions associated with the principle of ju. According to Draeger, one of martial arts' most experienced practitioners and prolific writers, there are two aspects of this underlying martial arts principle. The first part is the familiar yielding to strength to reduce or avoid the force of an opponent's attack. The second part is where yielding to strength is not possible. Resistance is an acceptable tool for a brief moment, after which an action of maximum efficiency or yielding will be executed. As Draeger notes, "It is the constant interplay of yielding and resisting that is the principle of ju and that makes Japanese methods of combat the dynamic systems that they are."

In another of Draeger's books, *Modern Bujitsu and Budo*, he relates that in Kano's mind, strength is an integral part of judo that must be utilized properly. The principle of maximum efficiency is the proper use of one's strength combined with the opponent's strength to enhance the effect of a technique. This idea negates the idea of judo being a defensive system. In Kano's judo, attack and defense are part of one another and are executed as simultaneous motions. Thus, judoka who are flexible in mind and body will be able to simultaneously dissipate or misdirect an opponent's force, use their strength as necessary, and execute a technique that combines the opponent's strength with their own. Used with the study of proper technique, movement, and timing, high-quality judoka can be developed in impressive numbers in a relatively short time. Once a judoka understands "giving way" and can apply it, conditioning, strategy, and other athletic attributes aforementioned will then enhance the judoka's abilities.

You can teach the principle of ju by carefully studying techniques and practicing their applications with cooperative moving throwing drills. Moving uchikomi and randori while blindfolded or with eyes closed is another good way to learn to feel your opponent's movement. In randori, discourage the use of strength, power gripping, and size as throwing tools. Tournament judo can be taught after the student has some understanding of giving way as a tool to defeat strength.

In ne waza, ju can be learned by practice utilizing only one hand against an opponent who is allowed to use both hands. Usually this opponent is of a lower skill level or lighter in weight. Another ne waza practice method is to practice with two opponents at the same time. Again, your opponents may be of lower skill level or lighter weight.

In later years, I had the privilege of working with Dr. Sashio Ashida, a master technician, who had a unique teaching style. He often spoke to us of the Zen conflict in learning ju. "Work hard, go easy," he would say with a smile. Dr. Ashida would spend hours in his clinics, teaching us the proper execution of techniques down to the minutest detail. In every lesson, he emphasized the principle of ju in performing the technique being studied.

Keep in mind the negative aspect of not teaching the principle of ju. Allowing incorrect posture, power gripping, and stiffness limits your students' true potential as technicians of judo. In addition, your injury rate is likely to increase. In his book, *The Canon of Judo*, the great Mifune, a tenth dan, stresses the Kodokan motto: "Utilize your energy to the best—this is the true meaning of judo."

Chapter 7

Some Ideas on Teaching Basics

In chapter 2, a brief outline was presented for basic judo instruction in the first one to three years. Now that the foundation has been established, it's time to expand and explain the outline further. The principles thus far discussed should be constantly emphasized with each phase of development.

Etiquette, hygiene, and history are of course up to the instructor, and many excellent resources are available to research correct bowing procedure and history. Hygiene is essential to prevent the spread of diseases and to make the workouts more pleasant for everyone. Fingernails and toenails must be kept short, and the mats and judogi must be kept clean to limit bacteria growth in the dojo.

Ukemi is an essential part of judo that protects us from injury and enables us to experience our partners' techniques without fear. Back falls are relatively easy to teach, as are side falls, providing you stress that the spine never touches the mat in a proper side fall. However, zenpo kaiten (rollouts) can be a traumatic experience for some students. When a student is afraid to launch his or her hips directly over his or her head, I recommend starting with a somersault, where both hands are placed in front of the shoulders, and the student supports his or her weight to push straight forward in a roll where the head never makes contact with the mat.

Once the somersault is satisfactory, try a rollout using the following procedure:

1) The student fully squats with the right foot slightly forward and places the left hand on the mat directly in front of the left shoulder.

2) Place the right hand on the mat diagonally across between the left hand and left foot, thus turning the right shoulder forward slightly.

3) The student then simultaneously lifts his or her hips, pushes with both legs over the right shoulder, and lands on the left side, slapping the mat with the left arm. Repeat on the other side.

Kuzushi 1

As the student gains confidence, have him or her bring the squat up a little higher each time and eventually remove his or her left hand from the mat. Most students probably can use more traditional methods, but this one works well with hesitant students. As your students get more skilled at rollouts, have them extend the motion and learn to throw themselves.

Another basic skill often neglected is the proper execution of forward kuzushi (off balancing). Breaking balance from a right-hand grip entails two basic motions simultaneously. As you step across with the right foot, the left, or sleeve hand, rotates the little finger upward as

Kuzushi 2

the arm draws the sleeve past tori's face. The head follows the wrist as you pull. This process is often called "opening your opponent up."

The right hand posts the collar up and forward while maintaining the elbow directly under the posting hand. (See photos.)

Teaching ne waza is not as clearly defined as teaching throwing. Most schools teach kesa gatame and a few other holds, then a series of chokes and escapes followed by arm bars when the student progresses a little.

I'm a bit more structured in my teaching of mat work. I've had good success dividing mat work into five or six beginning lessons. I teach two holds, usually kesa gatame and kami shiho gatame, in the first lesson. Then two escapes from these holds are taught in the second lesson. The third lesson follows with a little review and learning two turnovers when tori is on top of uke, who is on all fours. A week or so later, the student learns a choke or two, depending on his or her age and ability, usually hadaka jime and okuri eri jime, with legs around uke's legs from the rear. In another week or two, depending on student progress, the student is taught to transition from one hold to another and from a choke to a hold. The sixth lesson of the series then puts tori on his or her back to learn a turnover into a hold.

Using this series of lessons gives me a versatile student of mat work in about three or four months. I also find that this method helps prevent focusing on one technique too much. I do not recommend learning arm bars until the student is nearing brown belt (sankyu) level. As you can see, a lot of flexibility is built into these lessons to meet different student needs and abilities. Remember to stress technique over strength, and, of course, the principle of ju.

Throwing techniques are structured for us in the gokyo no waza. Why do so many judo schools teach osoto gari first? Well, let's see. The mechanics are relatively easy, control of the uke is simple, it requires minimum flexibility and athletic ability, and osoto gari is an awesome throw!

Many students can execute osoto gari in randori within a few weeks. Could ogoshi or seoinage be next? Of course, as they are a logical progression of the gokyo no waza.

Each throw requires an increase in skills and athletic ability, thus building balance and control. Also, the ultimate evil in judo skills is introduced: bending one's knees. Want to avoid problems before they start? Avoid teaching too much too soon. Being a keen observer of the "instant gratification" movement, especially in the United States over the past thirty years, I have repeatedly seen students who have learned techniques long before they were ready for them.

How many times have you seen a low-ranking judoka attempting uchi mata or sumi gaeshi? As a referee, I have seen many needless injuries because judoka learn these techniques too early in their judo development. In my mind, this type of teaching is irresponsible and unethical. I certainly would not want my children studying with this type of instructor.

The logical progression of the gokyo no waza helps us avoid these errors. Uchi mata is in the third kyo, and the student will probably be in judo at least two years and be sankyu or nikyu by the time uchi mata is reached in the progression. Is it okay to teach a throw in the third kyo to a student in his first year of judo? Instructor judgment comes into play here. Usually the answer is no, but occasionally superior athletes advance quickly.

What do you do with a student who picks up a technique that you feel is dangerous from a video or clinic? Tell him clearly that you feel he is not ready for this throw, and that he would be endangering himself and his partners to continue doing it. I usually throw in a little mystical, "I'll teach you when you're ready" to get them thinking about what being ready might entail.

As an example, I once had three thirteen- to fourteen-year-olds who were sankyu-level students attend a camp with the great Peter Seisenbacher. They came back from camp ready to try their new one-handed uchi matas. Since their judo was not yet world-class level and they were still learning uchi mata with two hands, I quickly curtailed the use of their new technique before someone got hurt.

Over the past four decades, I've listened to the advice of numerous instructors on how to develop quality judoka. Most of the time, the advice consisted of how to win in tournament. Attributes like hard work, not giving up, and hard randori dominated the conversations. However, the wiser instructors all seemed to be focused on developing certain skill sets in their students.

When discussing these skills with my own instructor, he told me that you could develop solid judoka in a relatively short period if you just taught your students to stand up straight, keep their feet under their shoulders, and bend their knees when entering for an attack. Another experienced sensei told me to focus on scoring ippon, rather than on just winning. Still another instructor told me that it was important to teach your students correct form before teaching them how to fight.

To these five basic ideas, I've added the skills of practicing without strength and sliding your feet when moving instead of stepping. Finally, I have always tried to teach that there is a correct time to make an attack that occurs when your opponent is most vulnerable. These eight basic skills and ideas combined can often successfully develop a very solid judoka in about one to three years.

Proper foot movement and placement are essential to good balance in judo as in any athletic activity. In judo, keeping your feet under your shoulders helps maintain optimum balance. When a judoka moves, sliding the feet instead of stepping makes him or her less susceptible to attack, especially from foot sweeps. Even many high-level competitors have the habit of crossing their feet when they move, making them potential foot-sweep victims. In tandem with learning proper footwork, a judo student should learn the basics of good ashi waza or foot techniques. Foot sweeps and reaps are great set-up throws, disrupt an opponent's timing, and are excellent weapons against opponents with poor footwork, often providing easy victories. Spend a considerable amount of time developing proper footwork, and you will be amazed at how often it makes a significant difference.

Teaching judo is a big responsibility. Chances to practice good judgment abound in every lesson. Take this responsibility seriously, remembering that an error in your judgment could result in a serious injury for someone else. Last, but certainly not least, keep the principle of ju foremost while teaching any technique. Timing a throw to take advantage of an opponent's strength or movement increases the possibility of success for a spectacular throw by a hundredfold.

Chapter 8

Teaching Children

Whether we realize it or not, teaching children is probably the most important part of teaching judo and running a dojo. These children are the future of judo, and they are the most impressionable and vulnerable of our students. If we don't realize that we instructors are role models every time we teach, we might negatively impact a youngster without intending to do so.

It is crucial that we understand how fragile egos can be for even the most obstinate teenagers. On the opposite end of the spectrum, it only takes one careless comment to shatter the self-esteem of a child who might have joined judo to gain confidence in the first place. The use of positive reinforcement in judo cannot be stressed enough. That six-year-old does not need to hear, "No, that's wrong, dummy." Simply change it to, "Let's fix this throw a little and make it work better for you."

To illustrate my point, I'd like to quote a few examples from an article in the United States Judo Federation publication, *JUDO Magazine* (Fall 2011, pages 35–36). The article, titled "Coaches Say the Darndest Things," by Connor Dantzler, uses quotes from various coaches as their young athletes remembered them. Below I have excerpted a few quotes that I feel best illustrate how callous and degrading coaches' remarks can be, especially in the excitement of competition. Imagine the possible negative effect on a youngster's self-esteem.

1) "You've got to stop getting down on yourself, you little jerk."
2) "It's just a broken thumb! You can still medal!"
3) "You know what second place is? It's first loser!"
4) "Bite him if you have to. Just don't leave a mark."
5) "You know, you guys have been working really hard, so it's not your fault you suck, just like last year."

Young athletes do not compete to intentionally lose. What would a coach possibly hope to gain from this type of coaching?

Another concern is, of course, safety. Children are resilient as a rule, due largely to their greater flexibility. However, certain techniques should probably wait until the child has the physical tools to perform them safely. The previously mentioned uchi mata is a good example. A poorly executed uchi mata is dangerous to both uke and tori and is the reason the "head dive" rule was instituted.

Morote seoinage can sometimes affect the elbows of young children much the same way as throwing a curveball in baseball does. In young children, the elbow has not yet reached maturity. I avoid morote seoinage until the student is about twelve to fourteen years of age, depending on the student's physical maturity level. Remember that once the elbow is damaged, there is no chance to start over. The child will either have a chronic elbow problem or need corrective surgery.

Being brutalized with an inappropriate pin or throw will discourage anyone, much less a child. Pair up students appropriately or with experienced students who will practice cooperatively with a less skilled partner. It's just another good way to teach mutual benefit! We could spend a long time on this topic, but the bottom line is that an instructor's good judgment and proper supervision is the key to safety. Any technique where the shoulder, knee, elbow, or especially the neck is exposed to violent impact or twisting should be avoided, especially with children. Save the riskier techniques of judo until they are mature enough to perform them properly.

The legal ramifications of running a dojo are a growing concern in teaching judo, especially with children. In the United States, lawsuits are all too common, even in unjustified situations. A proper release form, good mats, careful planning, liability insurance, written attendance, and sound teaching methods all help your dojo avoid and combat unpleasant legal scenarios.

However, a more serious problem has reared its ugly head in judo. A few cases of child molesters teaching our children judo have been documented. An instructor should carefully screen any potential assistant instructors for children's classes. Since no child molester is going to make it obvious what they are, it falls on the shoulders of the instructor to be acutely aware of any impropriety. Since judo is a hands-on activity, the instructor must ensure that any instructors or assistants not work with students in any manner that might be deemed inappropriate. In public education, teachers are warned not to meet with students behind closed doors, and if there is any doubt or concern about a student, have an adult witness present. Remember that if you are teaching a children's class alone, you have only your word to defend yourself in the case of any accusation. In this case, you might consider using a security camera to have a video recording of your classes.

In the worst-case scenario where one of your assistants is inappropriate with children in any way, including verbally, immediately remove the culprit from the class and your dojo. In extreme cases involving sexual abuse, have the person prosecuted. In the long run, it will protect other children as well as demonstrate your integrity. We now have background checks for all black-belt candidates in the United States, but a child molester could possibly slip under the radar.

Lastly, when disciplining children, make certain the discipline is appropriate for the behavior that you are addressing. Verbal abuse is not discipline! Identify the behavior that you want corrected, explain why it is inappropriate, and administer the appropriate discipline (in your judgment). Don't threaten! Threats do little to encourage good behavior, especially when you do not follow through on your threats.

I have found two techniques that work well. First, since most children love to participate in judo, sitting on the sideline for a while often improves the behavior. Second, telling the parents, with the child present, an explanation of the inappropriate behavior and why it can't be tolerated is usually very effective. Keep in mind that a child who repeatedly misbehaves is often seeking attention, even if it's negative attention. Let the child know that you like him or her but explain that the rules of the dojo are about everyone's safety and mutual benefit. Spend as little time with the incident as possible, handling it after class, if possible, when the student is not surrounded by his or her peers. Again, having an assistant who can take over while you deal with the child is a great asset. Make sure that the rules of the dojo are clear. Some dojos have their basic rules posted in the front of the dojo in a conspicuous location for students and parents to see. It is also a good idea to remind students periodically that what is learned in the dojo stays in the dojo. A call from the local school about a student using a choke on the playground usually means a bad day for everyone involved.

Most children (and adults) are visual learners, acquiring most information by watching someone demonstrate an activity or technique. Occasionally you may have a student, most likely a younger child, who does not appear to benefit from demonstration. You might even assume that this student is not paying attention to you. However, this student could be an auditory or possibly a tactile learner. Auditory learning is usually a learned behavior acquired at home or school and seldom presents an instructional problem, as it usually fits well with visual learning techniques. Tactile learners are often under ten years old and require special attention. To effectively learn, these students must have their hands, feet, and hips placed in the proper position for the technique being taught and may require repeated physical correction. Identifying a tactile learner early saves those students the frustration that might cause them to lose interest in judo. If you teach handicapped or autistic children, you will find tactile learning more frequently. We all use physical manipulation to correct technique with our students, but tactile learners require it constantly.

Children respond well to even the slightest positive recognition. Promotion certificates, small awards for hard work, verbal praise in front of their classmates, and their names in the newspaper after a shiai often keep interest in judo at a high level. One of the motivational tools we use is a poster called our Black Belt Hall of Fame. Once in a while, I'll point to it and tell the kids how great it will be to add their names to that list. It has provided a long-term goal for many students over the years.

Another avenue for fostering the children's interest and keeping them focused is the use of judo-related games. Since it is rare that a kid doesn't like to play games, it's a safe bet your classes will be more fun and will generate more interest if you include them in your curriculum. The following list will give you a few ideas for judo-related games.

1) Chicken fights: Make a ring of belts two to three meters in diameter. Two opponents remove their gi tops and bow. Each person grabs his or her own ankle with the same-side hand. The

object is to either push or pull the opponent outside the ring or cause him or her to touch the mat with any other part of the body other than the supporting foot. It's a great game for developing balance, body control, and, if you leave the gis on, better grips.

2) Sumo: Use a similar setup to chicken fights, except now children stand on both feet. After removing their gi tops (or not), the opponents try to force each other outside the ring or fall. Encourage the use of judo throws.

3) Rollouts over the belt: Practice rollouts jumping over an outstretched belt that two people hold. See who can clear the greatest height, jumping over the belt while executing a rollout. This game can be used for stretching rollouts lengthwise as well. Place soft objects on the mat, increasing the distance on each turn.

4) Knock down and out: A simplified randori game, where if any part of the body other than the person's feet touch the mat, they have to sit down. The winner gets to stay up to face a new challenger.

5) Shark attack: Mark off an area or use a crash pad about two meters square. Opponents on the pad try to push each other off the pad into the "shark-infested waters" around the pad. The game works best with three to four students at a time.

6) Card conditioning: On those slow days when only a few students show up for class, use a deck of cards with four jokers to decide some of their warm-up exercises. Shuffle the deck and spread them out facedown on the mat. Students take turns picking a card to decide their fates. For example, if the exercise is sit-ups, a student who draws an ace does one sit-up while a student drawing a king does thirteen sit-ups. When a student draws a joker, he or she does twenty-five sit-ups, and that exercise ends. The process is then repeated for push-ups, squat thrusts,

or any other part of your warm-up cycle. I have no idea why, but most kids love this game and will do it with their friends outside the dojo.

Consulting with other instructors can easily increase your game collection.

Chapter 9

Educating Parents

Parental involvement in your dojo can be either a great asset or a detriment to your instruction. Fortunately, most parents are well intentioned and want to support your program in any way possible. Parents have the right to be concerned about their children's progress, safety, and moral development. Most instructors learn the hard way about overzealous parents and parents who become judo experts without ever stepping on the mats. The problems might be coaching from the sidelines, pressuring for promotions, harassing referees at tournaments, or correcting techniques that you have taught based on something they saw or read somewhere. In contrast, helpful parents often act as tournament directors, fund-raisers, record keepers and timekeepers, or pool coordinators at tournaments.

Educating parents from day one will save you many nightmares later on. Discourage any type of coaching from the sidelines. Make parents understand that practice is just that—practice! Educate parents about judo etiquette and the goals of judo instruction. Many parents are caught up in the winning-or-losing model of sport. As you might expect, this phenomenon rarely occurs with parents who are themselves judoka. Assure these parents that there is much to gain from losing (getting thrown, pinned, etc.), especially the will to work harder. Don't forget to use your valuable parents as role models.

Over the years, I have seen the entire spectrum of parental behavior. One father put so much pressure on his son that I actually asked him to seek another dojo after he failed to reduce the emphasis on winning and being "the best." It might sound extreme, but the father simply could not tolerate his son's losing, even in the dojo. He could not seem to comprehend that being thrown and pinned were part of the judo learning process. (Yes, they left.)

I also made the mistake of allowing an aggressive mother to "encourage" a promotion for her daughter, even though I knew it was a bit premature. Soon after the desired promotion was awarded, the student stopped coming to practice. I'm certain that neither child nor parent learned anything about judo from me except that some instructors can be manipulated. At least I learned something valuable.

Another area of education for parents is nutrition. While many parents are extremely knowledgeable about proper rest and diet, others are not. I allow only water during practice and encourage students and their parents to avoid fast foods and sweets, especially before practice. With teenagers and young adults, I caution against using energy drinks that contain excessive amounts of caffeine and sugar. While I might appear altruistic, I'm actually trying to avoid weight problems, energy depletion, deficiency diseases, and problems like hyperactivity in my students.

Keeping parents informed is just part of preventive maintenance. Many times, adult students who have their own children in judo can counsel parents who have concerns about their children. Normally, even stubborn parents will change their views when they see that your methods lead to positive results in their children.

Chapter 10

Types of Practice

Depending on the variety of students in your dojo, you may want to offer separate classes for the advanced students or competitors. Most dojos have too few students for separate classes, and it limits the number of workout partners available. You might also want to have an open practice day for independent randori (supervised, of course). There are many ways to vary the type of practice in an individual lesson as well as in separate classes. In any case, use the flexibility of the lesson plan to help you organize. (see chapter 4)

Practice that helps break up the monotony of repetition and teaches or emphasizes different skills appears below:

1) Guided drills. These drills are instructor driven and available in many books, such as Ben Campbell's *Championship Judo Drill Training.*
2) Static drills. Usually for beginners, where one partner is still and cooperates while the other practices the mechanics of a technique.
3) Free movement drills. Tori and uke apply techniques on the move with one or both partners cooperating and working loosely. These drills are used to develop timing and position for throwing.

4) Randori. Free practice. Offense, defense, and counters are as relaxed as possible. Discourage the use of strength and size.

5) Speed uchikomi drills. Used to develop both speed and endurance. Push the limits by keeping a cadence a little above the student's physical ability.

6) Offense-defense. Tori is allowed to attack freely while uke may only defend without counters. This method allows tori to attack without fear or anticipation of counters. It also allows uke to concentrate on good defensive posture and movement.

7) Moving uchikomi or randori with eyes closed. Usually only one partner at a time closes his or her eyes, but only in a large area under instructor guidance. If the area permits, advanced students can both have their eyes closed with instructor supervision.

8) Club shiai. Class may be divided into two teams, or you may simply have individual matches. It is usually practiced with the instructor stopping the action to instruct. Dividing into teams can raise the level of excitement as well as reduce the focus on individual students. Keep it light and fun.

9) Regular shiai. Small tournaments can be approached as practice with pre- and post-shiai discussion including video, if possible. This approach may reduce the anxiety level for students. Sometimes this type of practice is done with one or two other clubs, with instructors allowed to stop action, as in the club shiai.

The intensity of practice should be geared to the physical and mental abilities of the students and their skill levels, age, and sometimes sex. Many dojos keep competition practice separate from regular classes to concentrate on shiai skills and reduce the emphasis on strength and gripping skills in the regular classes. Strenuous workouts on a regular basis can be discouraging for beginners, older judo students, and those not in good physical shape. Encourage students to gradually work up to full intensity.

Different clubs handle conditioning for judo in various ways. Some clubs leave it up to the individual, others include conditioning in class, while still others have regular conditioning sessions. Sometimes these sessions are part of competition training. Whether outside the dojo or in, try to keep it fun. Aim for constant movement with as much stretching and strength activity as possible mixed into the exercise. The object is for students to be exhausted, recover, and then repeat that process several times. Consult personal trainers for ideas, and then mix them in with judo drills. Keep in mind that every student has limits, so watch for heat exhaustion and dehydration. It is also wise to remind students that proper conditioning is a key factor in reducing the likelihood of injury. Judoka who are not in reasonable shape frequently suffer injuries that keep them off the mats.

You can change many aspects of judo, but one thing that never changes is the physics of judo. As soon as your students become adept at a technique, it is time to develop the speed at which they can perform it. It seems obvious that the faster you can execute a technique, the better the chance for success. This idea is hardly new in any athletic endeavor, but many instructors are not fully aware of how important speed development is in judo. After a student learns the proper form of a technique, he or she should practice until the movement is both smooth and fast. Speed becomes even more significant where great differences in size or strength exist.

In physics, Newton's third law shows that, put simply, the force of an action can be increased if you decrease the time executing that action.

net FORCE = mass X acceleration

note: acceleration = change in velocity / change in time

therefore: net Force = mass X change in velocity /

change in time

Judo practitioners refer (incorrectly) to this force as the power of the throw. It is fairly easy to see that as you decrease the change in time, the force of the action will increase proportionately when the mass and change in velocity remain constant (velocity normally increases, further enhancing the net force). In other words, if you can decrease the time to execute a technique by half, you will double the force of that technique! So skipping the math and science, an instructor should emphasize speed practice once a technique has been properly learned.

This way, smaller or weaker judoka can be successful against larger or stronger opponents. In the final analysis, the real test of your judo ability is how well you fare against these bigger, stronger opponents. Many of the great masters of judo have been slight of build but were able to defeat much larger and stronger opponents with their combination of speed and skill. Make speed practice part of your program, especially with more advanced students.

Chapter 11

Special Needs Judo

Nearly twenty years ago, I had a young lady with cerebral palsy join my dojo. One arm and one leg were severely impaired, but her spirit soared above all her physical problems. She became an inspiration for all her fellow judoka, as she refused special treatment and tried to do everything she was taught. It was my first experience teaching a grueling physical activity to someone with such severe limitations. She soon convinced me that anything was possible if you just refused to give up.

A few years later, one of my black belts approached me about starting a judo class at the area Children's Annex, a school for special needs children that specialized in treating autism. His son attended the school for a couple of years and had been practicing judo in our children's classes. Having seen the improvement in his son, he came up with the idea of a special needs judo class. I thought about it and recalled the previously mentioned young lady who had reminded me that kids with handicaps do not get picked for teams and have limited opportunities in sport. So my answer was, "Why not?" If there's one great thing about judo, it's that everyone gets to play!

To make a long story short, the program has flourished and spread to our dojo in a class designed to continue to teach special needs children after they become too old for the school setting. Our program is now international, with a few of our students traveling to Italy and Wales to compete in special needs tournaments. It turns out that Europe has a well-organized special needs program with an annual shiai and clinic in Ravenna, Italy.

In 2008, our dojo hosted Mr. Roy Court and his special needs team from Wales. They practiced all week with us, and Roy gave a clinic on the organization of special needs judo in Europe. The skills these students displayed were impressive, but the most noteworthy thing was the spirit and enjoyment that they exhibited in every practice. At present, the United States is way behind in this aspect of judo, with the exception of classes for the visually impaired.

Looking back over the years, we have learned a great deal from teaching special needs children. First, we found that, given time, patience, and instruction, autistic children could acquire good basic judo skills. The parental support for special needs judo is fantastic! Organizations for autistic children are willing to support and fund programs for their kids. Autistic children look forward to practice and usually have excellent attendance. The benefits for autistic children that we documented were increased confidence, improved motor skills and posture control, improved tolerance for others, improved concentration, and increased sensory awareness. Many displayed a noticeable decrease in touch sensitivity, a common condition with autistic children.

Close monitoring is required so frustration won't erupt into angry outbursts and to prevent occasional bullying. One instructor or assistant with every pair of special needs students is ideal because it allows you to immediately correct technique or behavior and remedy lack of attention.

Be prepared for the unexpected as special needs students often have their own interpretations of things. One such event occurred in a small special needs tournament that we held for our class. The shiai pitted the special needs team against our adult judo class, who had graciously donated their time. As the shiai progressed, each student got to experience a contest match with an adult from our club as an opponent and myself as the referee.

One young girl apparently was studying me intently. When it was her turn, she attacked her opponent and received a koka for a score. As I awarded the score with my hand signal, she abruptly turned and gave me a high five. The entire place erupted in laughter. Of course, the unexpected events aren't always this humorous.

Before starting a special needs judo program, make sure to talk to professionals about the requirements for teaching special needs children. You'll need plenty of help, especially if the class is bigger than five or six students. Patience takes on a whole new meaning, and your discipline has to be firm, fair, and low key. Guidelines need to be clearly defined with constant reinforcement. Despite all the concerns, the rewards far outweigh the negatives. Get used to seeing frequent smiles and unbridled joy when you award a promotion.

Chapter 12

Plan for the Future

Whenever you open a dojo, the furthest thing from your mind is the future of your club. Instead, you are more focused on the club's survival. Just as it is important for judo players to set goals for their personal judo, it is important for an instructor to establish goals for the dojo. One of the first goals I set for my club was to develop ten young shodans to hopefully carry on judo instruction in the future.

My dojo has been in existence for nearly forty years. Before that, the club went through an evolution for about six years that eventually combined three separate clubs and a series of instructors and assistants. This longevity is due more to good fortune, however, than to good planning. The main reason our doors are still open is a good reputation as a place to learn solid judo basics at an affordable price. The second reason for our success is a solid base of loyal and dedicated ranking students who adhere to the principles taught and who assist me as I get older and less able to do the actual training.

Looking back, I realize that teaching your students to give back to judo is critical to the very existence of judo. The day eventually comes when an instructor can no longer do everything that a dojo requires because of age, injury, or life circumstances. Chapter 4 explored becoming a competent instructor. You can develop such people in your classes over the years. Share your methods of instruction with anyone who shows an interest. Encourage ranking students to recall what it was like to be a beginner and have them assist with lower ranks. When your competitors retire, ask them to assist and eventually take over a class. This process can be done individually or as a team effort with several potential instructors. Be cognizant of people who work better with adults than children or vice versa. To ensure quality instruction, have them focus on clarity of communication and continuity of instruction. Teach them how to create and utilize lesson plans.

As soon as possible, begin building an instruction team in your dojo. This team should be as highly skilled as possible and committed to teaching the same things the same way. Once you have a team in place, you have people to take the lead if you have to be away or are injured. Have various members lead warm-ups, teach falling, and introduce entry-level techniques. Always capitalize on the individual strengths of your team members.

As time goes on, encourage some of your advanced black belts who have retired from competition to open dojos in areas where there is little or no judo. As you get older, look for someone to take over for you when you decide to retire or curtail your involvement. It is never too soon to instill the idea that we reap many benefits from judo and that someone has to provide the leadership for judo to exist and grow. "Giving back to the sport" is a phrase often used but too seldom seen. Fortunately for judo, there are enough of us to keep things going. The problem has been that many of the people willing to run dojos are relatively inexperienced, especially in the teaching department. Imagine where judo instruction would be today if the dedicated disciples of Dr. Kano had not relocated in other countries to help the spread of judo!

The future of a dojo also depends on location and economics. A club that changes location frequently usually loses students each time. Likewise, a club that charges high tuition relative to the economic status of the area will discourage students who simply cannot afford the expense of judo.

I have observed that many clubs offer working scholarships for economically challenged students. These students are entrusted with the hygiene and upkeep of the dojo as well as assisting with the organization and record keeping for tournaments. They sometimes are also given fund-raising responsibilities. Occasionally parents or businesses will sponsor a student who does not have enough money for judo classes.

The more that students realize that judo does not have to end with competitive retirement, the more likely they are to remain involved with judo. Training in kata, refereeing, coaching, and as judo support personnel all provide opportunities for judo players to remain involved after their competition careers are over.

Chapter 13

The Spirit of Judo

Once during a discussion with my ranking students about what originally attracted us to judo, one of my senior students, Bill Scribner, commented, "I was impressed that it was even more important *how* you won. Sometimes how you won was *more important* than the winning itself." This comment was and still is one of the best observations I've heard on the spirit of judo. Often vague and esoteric, the spirit of judo has frequently been used to describe and support any question about judo that requires more than a one-word answer.

The spirit of judo embodies a multitude of desirable human qualities, like honesty, sportsmanship, tenacity, citizenship, sacrifice, and commitment. Most of the judo teachers in my life have attempted to place judo on a higher plane than most other human activities. Judo is often referred to as an art; an educational system for the mind, body, and spirit; a martial art sport; self-esteem development; and an honor system. Stories and visions of samurai lore sometimes cloud the meaning rather than clarify it.

Whatever your interpretation, there is little doubt that judo is much different from that first glimpse of two people grappling in their pajamas. As we progress in judo technique and understanding, more is expected of us. We are encouraged to represent judo in a good light, give back to judo, and become more humble the farther we advance. One of my women students once commented about a high-ranking judoka teaching a clinic, saying, "He's one of the toughest guys on the planet, but he shows no arrogance and goes out of his way to make sure nobody gets hurt—a real gentleman." This comment sums up my experience with most of the experts in judo that I have encountered. They are skilled beyond what seems to be maximum human potential, modest to the point of shyness, and concerned with other people's progress and welfare on and off the mat. The spirit of judo lives on in many of its disciples.

Chapter 14

Keeping a Balance of Instruction

If you are a traditionalist in judo instruction, the scope of what you are responsible for teaching can be overwhelming. The instructor is expected to cover history, physical fitness, philosophy, etiquette, tachi waza, ne waza, competition, kata, and self-defense as well as a little hygiene, first aid, and psychology. Dr. Kano described judo in the following manner: "Judo is the way to the most effective use of both mental and physical strength. Training you in attacks and defenses refines your body and soul and helps you make the spiritual essence of judo a part of your very being. In this way, you are able to perfect yourself and contribute something of value to the world. This is the final goal of judo discipline."

I've seen this quote many times, and it always amazes me when I analyze it. Perfecting myself is still a work in progress in my life, especially if you ask my family. Contributing something of value to the world is a higher order accomplishment in my way of thinking. While I'm working on myself, am I expected to teach others how to accomplish the *final* goal too? Suddenly I feel inadequate!

Of course, judo is more than a one-semester course, and to learn all that Judo encompasses is probably at least a lifelong study. Keep in mind that many early Japanese instructors dedicated their lives to judo and normally did little else but train and teach. Their students took care of their everyday needs. Today's instructors usually have to hold real jobs to support their families and seldom have the luxury of daily training. Therefore, to achieve a balance of instruction, a teacher must incorporate the various aspects of judo into his or her lessons. If you have a student for four years, you can include plenty of history, philosophy, and etiquette along with the technical instruction.

One of my favorite techniques for incorporating different aspects of judo in a lesson is storytelling, often before or after the actual lesson. For example, one of my favorite stories for teaching sportsmanship and humility is about a young American I met who trained in Japan for years and returned to the United States to compete in the nationals. He shall remain nameless as I do not have permission to use his name, but he dazzled the crowd with his repertoire of techniques as he fought his way to the finals, each match ending with ippon. In the finals, his opponent received a keikoku penalty (half point) for stepping outside the mat area, a huge lead at that point in the match. Feeling that winning by penalty was not an honorable victory, this classy judoka stuck his foot forward, got foot swept, and took a perfect wazari fall, thus tying the score. The rest of the match was scoreless, and he lost a close referees' decision. A national championship was not as important as sportsmanship and honor. The appreciative crowd gave him an ovation as he humbly bowed and left the mat.

In summary, you can plan the peripheral lessons of judo around and in between your technical instruction. Don't be concerned with doing it all at once. Remember, the path is the goal!

Chapter 15

Things I Learned from the Greats

Recently I attended a clinic with the fabulous Kosei Inoue. When I returned home, I pondered what I had left the clinic with to add to my "bag of tricks." I was surprised to find that the three things that impressed me most with this man were his patience, humility, and emphasis on correct kuzushi (off balancing). I might add his uchi mata wasn't too bad either. The following list of ideas is taken from my notes on the many clinics and seminars I have attended over the years. Some of them may appear vague and probably need further explanation, but you'll get the gist of it. Besides, you will create your own list over time.

M. Swain—you are champion for a day!

Ms. Fukuda—there really is gentleness in judo.

T. Kidachi—the essence of timing.

Y. Yonezuka—true leadership.

S. Oishi—first form, then fight.

N. Adams—correct double lapel turnover.

I. Inokuma—make your favorite technique unstoppable.

J. Pedro—escape from leg entanglement.

K. Shiina—the importance of a proper bow.

N. Ogasawara—patience and how to play smart.

M. Eguchi—never give up.

T. Dalton—call 'em as you see 'em

A. Parisi—attack the open space.

Y. Yamashita—the versatility of ouchi gari.

S. Ashida—too numerous to mention, but mostly that judo and life are full of Zen conflicts.

H. S. Han—coaching competitors to win by being opportunistic (situational judo).

K. Takata—the application of kata to randori.

T. Sengoku—"If you're going to be a tree, be a willow, not an oak."

Professor Kudo—the importance of practicing with as little strength as possible.

Chapter 16

Competition

If you recall, the scope of this book is for instructors wishing to develop a well-rounded basic judo program for the proliferation of quality judo. The focus is not on international competition but rather on the development of sound judo technique and a thorough understanding of judo's underlying principles.

However, competition is an integral part of any quality judo program. While competition may not be for all judoka, students who are capable of competing should be encouraged to participate in shiai. Competition provides an opportunity to test one's skill development and mental discipline. While winning is certainly more satisfying than defeat, losing is often more instructive. Flaws in one's judo frequently become apparent in competition. Thus, competition is of great value to an instructor in evaluating a student's technical progress.

It is most important for an instructor to emphasize that the value of competition encompasses much more than the opportunity to perform quality judo under a stressful situation. Competition also fosters humility, a fighting spirit, respect for one's opponents, and sportsmanship. After the contest is over, analyzing film and discussing strategy and developmental needs enhance the value of the experience.

My own instructor told us that the most important thing about competition was showing up. Anyone can stay home or choose not to compete. It takes character to stand alone on the line across from an opponent.

Children and adults both may exhibit apprehension about entering competition. People often equate losing with being inadequate or unacceptable. An instructor who is patient and supportive with students will find that sooner or later they will want to test the waters. Students who are taught competition basics often feel a bit more relaxed about entering competition. Fundamentals such as cross-gripping, controlling the power arm (right arm on a right-sided player), and circular movement to combat stiff arms will give novice competitors things to focus on rather than those butterflies in their stomachs.

In today's competitive judo, gripping is an essential skill that many times consumes the majority of a match. Getting one's grip quickly and efficiently is certainly a bonus for any competitor. Since there are several excellent books about gripping, I won't repeat what you may already know and can easily read elsewhere. However, it is essential that students learn to get a comfortable grip and use it to throw their opponents instead of stalling. In ne waza, the goal is usually to grip and control the arm and shoulder or the leg and hip of your opponent. Arm locks especially require control of the wrist and elbow joints for consistent success, not gripping the sleeve of the gi for control.

It is important to teach more advanced competitors how to change directions with their attacks. Combinations like kouchi gari to ouchi gari or kouchi gari to uchi mata give competitors an edge in defeating opponents with strong defense. Encourage students to do what they have been taught and to do their best. Stress the excitement and camaraderie that judo competition fosters, and concentrate on team performance where possible rather than on individual achievement. Remind successful students that today's victors often are tomorrow's losers and vice versa.

An instructor's use of positive reinforcement almost always lifts the spirits of a student who has had a tough day on the mats. Find something positive to focus on!

I have two basic rules for competition in our dojo:

1) Do not go into competition out of shape. The only real negative outcome of a contest is injury.
2) Enter competition with a positive attitude. There are things to be learned and gained regardless of the outcome. Participate to learn and have fun.

A major concern of many competitors is weight management. An athlete's optimum competition weight is usually considerably lower than his or her normal weight. Often competitors get into the bad habit of starving themselves to get to the next lower weight division, emulating their wrestling cousins. Discourage this practice as it is unhealthy, especially during the growth years, and can lead to many physical problems, including needless injuries. Encourage proper rest and nutrition and maintaining a healthy weight for their ages and body builds. If you are lucky enough to have a doctor, nurse, or nutritionist in your dojo, you can have them help you address competitors plagued with maintaining weight.

Competition is also a great place to do some goal setting with your more serious competitors. Below is a rough outline I use with my students when they have experienced some competition and show an interest in higher-level challenges. Although there is no specific timetable for this type of coaching, I have usually found that students are in the ikkyu to nidan range in rank. This outline covers the minimum requirements for higher-level (national or above) competition:

Judo Competition Requirements

    I)   Skills—basics
        A. Throws
           1) One front
           2) One rear

3) One opposite side
B. Mat work—emphasis on pinning and transitions
C. Posture
D. Grips
E. Timing
F. Defense and counters

II) Conditioning
A. Cardio
B. Speed
C. Strength
D. Flexibility
E. Diet
F. Optimum weight

III) Strategy
A. Competition rules
B. Position on the mat
C. Fakes and combinations
D. Mental preparation

IV) Preparation
A. Setting goals
a. Long term
b. Short term
B. Focus—one step at a time
C. Building confidence
D. Sacrifice and commitment

V) The Big Picture
A. Level of competition
B. When to move up
C. Enjoyment
D. When to hang it up

This outline is individualized for each competitor and updated as the student advances. If expectations and ability progress satisfactorily, there may come a time when I suggest that the student train at a larger dojo or at a training center.

In the book *The Fighting Spirit* of Judo by Yasuhiro Yamashita, his coach Nobuyuki Sato offers some insight into coaching strong competitors in his postscript to the text. Of special note is his advice on goal setting. He lists five points that I have summarized below:

1) To give better students harder training than average students.
2) To gradually increase the difficulty of training.
3) To continue training for an extended term where appropriate.
4) To let players understand the purpose and effects of training so that they can practice confidently.
5) To find a suitable method for each player, and not concentrate on a single method.

Note the emphasis on individualization of training (point 5). Sato also mentions that arrogance is a serious obstacle to progress and that teaching competitors requires that they also learn how to apply what they have learned from judo to the rest of their lives. In other words, judo training is about not only winning medals but also becoming a person of integrity who thinks for himself or herself.

Training students for competition should also include a thorough explanation of the contest rules of judo. As a referee, I have always been amazed at the number of coaches that do not fully understand the rules or have their own personal interpretations. Strategy is involved in judo competition, as it is with all sports. For example, stalling when you have a lead can quickly get you into penalty trouble and soon erase your lead. A good strategy is to teach your competitors to keep the pressure on their opponents, even when they are ahead. Your students should understand that many of the rules in judo are designed to protect the competitors from injury. Many times a referee may stop an action at a critical point because in his or her judgment there is some danger to one or both opponents. All referees make mistakes, but arguing with a referee is a huge tactical error. There is a correct procedure for discussing a perceived error on the referee's part.

In conclusion, as an instructor, you are a role model for your students. Rest assured that what you say and do will be emulated. If you and your students know the rules and conduct yourself in a respectful manner, your dojo will be respected and treated fairly.

Chapter 17

Kata

For years, I've listened to the arguments about teaching and practicing kata. Many top coaches and competitors have voiced objections, stating that the practice of kata is too time consuming with too little benefit, especially for competitors. Proponents of kata say that it improves technical ability and timing, and teaches how to set up techniques. The argument goes on and on, often becoming heated when there are kata requirements for promotion.

I don't claim to be a kata expert, but I have trained with Dr. Ashida, Mr. Takata, Mr. Sengoku, and Ms. Fukuda, just to mention a few. I'm comfortable with a few katas and at one time or another have practiced all the katas. I can honestly say that kata has improved every aspect of my own judo, especially left side throws and armlocks. I can also say that kata has done no harm to my judo and that I've gained a greater appreciation of the scope of judo training.

Many people have the impression that kata is for high-ranking judoka only and involves techniques beyond the abilities of average judoka. In my experience, kata is more about practicing basic movements and principles. Most brown belts have enough judo skills to begin learning some kata. If nothing else, the practice of kata provides good low-impact exercise and a break from the rigors of training. For injured or older judoka, kata provides a way to stay active and involved when competition is not feasible.

In the long term it is up to the instructor and the local ranking organization, if any, just how much kata should be taught. Both sides have reasonable concerns, and it seems that a reasonable compromise can be reached. High-level competitors, national level or higher, probably should spend less time on kata and come back to it when their competition days are over.

Finding time to teach kata can often be frustrating, especially when your dojo is preparing for tournament. Learning kata is time consuming and requires going to clinics. However, there is no rush. It can take years to become proficient in a kata. Make a decision on how well rounded you want your students to be in their judo knowledge and just do your best. The answer to your question is yes. I teach kata classes and am pleased with the results.

Chapter 18

Self-Defense

In the United States, insurance companies have required that judo organizations change the focus of judo to that of a sport instead of a martial art. Liability and avoiding litigation are the driving forces instead of tradition and knowledge. Our national organizations have cautioned us against teaching self-defense and any techniques that might not be covered under our insurance in an injury claim. Living in the land of lawyers and litigation, US judo instructors live under the constant threat of lawsuits for negligence of any type, whether real or not.

Of course, an instructor should be held accountable for negligence, but I'm sick of insurance companies dictating what can be taught or not taught in judo. Most students have their own medical insurance, and the insurance coverage for judo is mediocre at best. The liability insurance provided is rarely ever needed but is an asset for a dojo. After all, judo is a contact activity, and injuries do occur. I've been told that it's a necessary evil and that I should not teach self-defense any longer or should disguise it well. What's an instructor to do?

Judo comes from jujutsu, the sole purpose of which is maiming or disabling an opponent when you are attacked. I see nothing wrong with defending yourself. Many students are attracted to judo for its value as a self-defense tool. Let's remember that judo is an eclectic composition of techniques, most of which were taken from the three jujutsu masters that Dr. Kano studied under. Professor Kano modified and removed some jujutsu techniques to make judo safer for everyone to practice as well as to make judo an activity for mutual benefit instead of mutual mayhem.

Self-defense can still be included in judo in several ways. First, self-defense is part of the judo katas, which can be practiced as kata, not self-defense. Self-defense instruction can be moved out of the dojo to another location with no affiliation to your judo program, and of course, with no insurance either. Lastly, teaching armlocks, chokes, and throws as an opponent reaches for your gi or changes grips are applicable to self-defense while still covered under judo competition skills. With a little ingenuity, you can incorporate some self-defense training in your judo program.

Chapter 19

Injuries and First Aid

All physical activities have risks, and judo is certainly no exception. The most important part of dojo management and class instruction is injury prevention. Safe mats, good falling technique, and sensible practice rules will prevent many injuries. The rest of the injuries fall under the realms of accident or carelessness, and you must be prepared to deal with them.

First, you must keep a well-stocked first-aid kit, including antiseptic, bandages, tape, tweezers, scissors, arm and leg splints, antibiotic cream, ace bandages, and of course, ice! Be especially careful administering pain relievers because many people may have allergies to them, and never give pain medication to children. Take a basic first-aid course and a CPR course and learn especially what NOT to do! Treating an injury and making it worse is a crime of ignorance. If you don't know how to treat it, call someone who does know. Serious injuries require immediate attention, so a phone should be available to call emergency numbers. If you have trained medical personnel in your dojo, let them do what you cannot.

One aspect of judo that especially frightens spectators is when someone loses consciousness while being choked. While there is little danger for a healthy individual, some simple guidelines can help avert a serious situation. First, no person with high blood pressure, a heart condition, or a history of stroke should ever be choked. If a student does pass out in a choke, simply sit the person up and gently spread the shoulders to allow air into the lungs and normal blood flow to the brain. At this point, he or she will usually come around. If they do not, immediately check for breathing. Convulsions can cause a person to swallow his or her tongue and choke. Since a convulsing person is difficult to sit up, make sure that the tongue is clear and roll the person on his or her side, facing at a downward angle. Keep them under mild restraint to prevent injury. The convulsions normally stop in a few seconds as the person regains consciousness. Some students may experience some nausea or dizziness, especially if it's the first time that they have passed out. The main thing to remember is not to panic. Choking is not dangerous for healthy individuals under normal practice conditions.

Of paramount concern in the dojo is preventing the spread of infectious diseases. From athlete's foot and the common cold to hepatitis and staph infections, it is important to stop communicable diseases immediately, or better yet, prevent them in the first place. The easiest place to start is with a clean dojo.

- The mats, bathrooms, and changing rooms must be kept clean and disinfected. Discourage the sharing of water bottles, judogis, and towels.
- Students who appear ill or lacking proper hygiene should be kept off the mats until the situation is remedied.
- Keep antibacterial soap in the bathroom and a bottle of hand sanitizer conspicuously located near the mats.
- Also keep a bleach solution on hand in case of bleeding. Dispose of any medical waste properly.
- Remind students that vaccinations for diseases like hepatitis B are available.

- Encourage your students to stay home when they feel ill and to seek medical attention if necessary, to ensure everyone's wellbeing.

Two adults should be present at all times in children's classes. Two heads are better than one, four hands are better than two, and one of you might be the injured person. In the case of bleeding, one person can suppress the bleeding while the other calls for help. There is no substitute for knowledge and having an action plan in the event of an injury. Lastly, a good idea is keeping a medical reference manual in the dojo. After you have read it, place it on a shelf for quick reference in situations that may not be familiar to you. In the dojo I keep a first-aid manual and a copy of Anthony Catanese's book on the medical care of judoka. (See bibliography.)

Chapter 20

Dojo Pride and Motivation

Did you ever receive a gold star on your homework in school? Most children respond positively to recognition and praise. So do adults. In judo we have a ranking system to recognize progress, hard work, and dedication. Nothing motivates like a well-earned, well-timed promotion.

Many other motivational tools are available to instructors that provide recognition, establish a sense of pride in your dojo, and encourage students to persevere when they are having difficulty. Many dojos have award ceremonies for presenting rank, especially black-belt ranks. Certificates and medals for judoka, especially children who may not be winning in tournaments, encourage them to continue. A bulletin board with pictures and newspaper articles of successful students is another great motivator. Plenty of clubs have websites with information and pictures of their students. Our dojo has a Black Belt Hall of Fame, with the names of all students who have achieved dan ranking over the years posted conspicuously in the front of the dojo. Most clubs these days have team sweat suits and T-shirts, displaying their club affiliations as well as club designs embroidered on their judogis.

Chapter 21

Sensei or Coach?

Much has been written about the true meaning of "sensei" and what constitutes the difference between a coach and a sensei. I only include a chapter on the topic in this book to help prospective judo instructors clarify their roles. As an educator, I have coached elementary, modified, JV, and varsity football, as well as wrestling and girls' basketball. As a judo instructor, I believe that I started as a coach and later became a sensei. Since I have experienced both avenues of involvement, I feel that I have some expertise on the topic.

When you read the literature and dictionary definitions of the two terms, you quickly realize there are numerous overlapping areas in the coach-sensei discussion. While coaches are quick to point out the similarities of the two terms, there are two glaring differences between a coach and a sensei. Those differences are culture and length and depth of involvement with the students.

In my judo studies over the past forty years, some of my instructors have emphasized that a sensei must embrace his or her responsibilities for developing the total person: body, mind, and spirit. The perfection of human development is a tall order, but it appears to be what Dr. Kano had in mind when he organized his judo plan. The word "sensei" has been explained to me as one who has mastered a set of skills to the point that he or she can successfully teach those skills to others in hopes of passing on those skills.

The word "sensei" in Japan is not reserved for martial arts instructors but can refer to anyone who has developed skills beyond the norm in any human activity. In several dojos that I have attended, if the instructor was sixth dan or above, he or she was referred to as "shihan" instead of "sensei." To me, this term indicated a higher order of skills, beyond that of most senseis—a sort of top ten percent of all judoka who have become instructors.

On Neil Ohlenkamp's Judo Information website, he states the word "sensei" literally translates as "one who has gone before." My instructors have often related their "long journeys" in judo to me. They have also spent a great deal of time, especially with their ranking students, developing character and judo spirit as well as technical and competitive skills. This appreciation of judo culture and history takes years and is often taught outside the dojo in diners, at parties, and sometimes in actual classrooms.

In contrast, coaches usually spend roughly from one to four years with their athletes, while senseis normally spend from four to ten years with many of their students just as competitors. After that, many judoka spend years beyond competition still studying with their senseis, expanding their judo knowledge and appreciation. Certainly coaches teach many valuable skills and values, but the ultimate goal is winning. To a judo sensei, winning is only a small part of judo education. Often losing is viewed as equally or even more valuable in judo development.

Imagine a high school or college football or baseball coach who invests twenty years with his most dedicated players. It simply is not in the nature of a competitive sport such as football or baseball to maintain relationships for this amount of time, except on a rare occasion. Again, coaches spend more time on winning and the fundamentals necessary to achieve victory. Why, you ask? Often the coaches' jobs depend on whether they consistently win or not.

I had the privilege of knowing one of US judo's finest senseis. Ralph Reyes, who passed away a short time ago, was one of the most respected senseis in the nation. His many quality students are a testimonial to his abilities as a teacher of judo. Their dedication and love for their sensei illustrate that he was more than just a guy teaching judo techniques to win. When you talk to Ralph's students about him, they seldom speak of how he made them champions. Instead they tell of how he bailed them out of a jam, guided them in the right direction, took them to a tournament with his own money, or mediated a family dispute. In addition to running a dojo, Ralph also refereed extensively and often took junior teams abroad to compete at a moment's notice. As a friend and colleague, Ralph embodied what I view as a sensei, total involvement and a commitment to improving and enriching the lives of his students.

Coaches and senseis both are of great value in society. They both provide valuable skills and experiences in human development. There are great coaches and senseis, and there are less-than-great coaches and senseis as well. As a judo instructor, you need to decide what level of involvement you want in your dojo. Do you want to be a judo coach or a judo sensei? Both paths entail responsibility and dedication, but a sensei will ultimately be much more closely involved with his or her students. A sensei will eventually have a huge "family of judoka," many of whom he or she has helped outside of judo.

By the way, in my years of coaching, I saw several coaches develop beyond the winning agenda and become senseis of their own sports. They expanded their teaching philosophies beyond what is normally expected of a coach and became concerned with the total development of their athletes. Coaches are often limited by time and the institutions that employ them, so they have less time and opportunity to develop into senseis.

Chapter 22

When Should I Open a Dojo?

Opening a dojo requires you to have a fair amount of time to donate to judo. Between career and family commitments, most people simply do not have sufficient time to properly run a dojo. If you cannot clear at least three nights per week in your schedule, you should probably wait, or assist in another dojo.

Second, make sure that you secure a good location, adequate mats, adequate ventilation, and insurance prior to teaching classes. This might sound like common sense, but many dojos start out as classes at a local community center, where they might remain or move out to a private location. Often these organizations do not cover individual programs under their community insurance plans.

In Japan, judo instructors are trained and are normally fifth dan and above, indicating a high skill level and many years of experience. In other countries, this level may not always be possible, and lower ranks (skill levels) may have to run judo clubs. This is not to say that lower-ranking instructors cannot develop quality students; it's just more likely with more experienced and skilled instructors.

I am convinced that first-degree black belt is *not* a sufficient rank for someone to become an instructor. However, I have seen many dojos with shodans and even brown belts as instructors. In areas with very little judo, inexperienced people may find themselves in the instructor role. I know because it happened to me. This situation may work if that person is smart enough to seek experienced guidance and continue to improve his or her own judo in that process.

So, you've secured your location. You have achieved a level where you feel comfortable instructing classes. You have the spare time. What else do you need to make the big move? Commitment! There will be dozens of times when your personal life, professional life, and judo life will conflict. Successful judo programs are like any other activities. They require continuity of instruction, consistency of practice, and the instructor's determination to let nothing interfere with that process. Don't be discouraged. Someone has to do it. It might as well be you. Keep an open mind, and continue your own growth in judo and teaching skills. If you do a decent job, the rewards will be numerous but probably not monetary.

Chapter 23

The Rewards

The teaching of judo offers several benefits that may be overlooked in the beginning of starting a dojo. The simple satisfaction of knowing that you have done a reasonably good job at helping people attain goals that they may never have achieved on their own is a good start. On the practical side, there is little reason to belong to a gym when you teach judo. There is ample opportunity to keep in shape and get the exercise your body needs to remain healthy.

As an instructor, you also get to meet some very talented people, both physically gifted and intelligent. At times you provide the structure and direction to guide people on a positive path in life. This guidance is especially significant when it provides children with positive goals and motivates them to persevere during difficult times. After you have taught for about twenty years, you begin to receive compliments from former students on how you helped them make productive choices and stay focused in life. The downside is that sometimes you receive these compliments through their children or grandchildren, reminding you that you're not as young as you once were.

If you are actively involved in the various phases of judo, you will undoubtedly do a significant amount of traveling to some very interesting places, where you will meet even more talented people. Your cultural appreciation and development will increase dramatically as you realize how many talented people are associated with judo. Perhaps the most valuable gift teaching judo provides is the constant learning and improving that accompanies instruction. Countless experiential lessons can keep you creative and motivated to improve not only your students but also yourself.

Once again, the path is the goal!

Think about what judo teaches us. It teaches respect, self-discipline, perseverance, physical fitness, hygiene, appreciation of other cultures, and mental efficiency. Who wouldn't feel rewarded by passing on some of these assets to the quality of human life?

Chapter 24

Final Thoughts

To those of you who decide to run a dojo, I wish you nothing but success. The future of judo is with you and your students. I feel a few things should be emphasized as you teach your students:

1) Try to remember how you felt the first day you stepped on the mat or the first time you competed. Judo can be very stressful on your ego, and self-confidence can be destroyed as well as developed.

2) Put as much fun in practice as possible. Judo is a grueling sport, and the people you train with and teach need to enjoy practice if they are going to stay with it.

3) Make practice as safe as possible. No one comes to judo class looking for an injury. The discipline of the dojo must include mutual respect and care from the senior students for the lower ranks.

4) Keep an open mind. Judo is an international activity, and there are many correct ways to develop good judoka.

5) Teach effective judo. Students who cannot control untrained opponents lose interest quickly, and besides, why take judo if it doesn't work? Teach what you know well. Seek assistance on techniques that

you are not proficient in demonstrating or teaching.

6) Learn when to send your students other places to train. Top-level judoka need to be exposed to many techniques and many opponents. Few instructors are well versed in all the various techniques of judo.

7) Be patient. Learning takes time, and everyone learns at different rates. Refrain from yelling at your students. If you are frustrated, walk away.

8) Teach respect, and be a role model for your students.

9) Never ask your students to do anything that you wouldn't do yourself.

10) Remain humble. As you progress in judo and advance in rank, it is difficult not to become somewhat egotistical about what you have attained and jaded about what other people may not know. High rank and teaching success may be accompanied by an air of superiority and arrogance. If for no other reason, remember that you will always be a role model for your students and younger instructors. Humility is at the very root of judo philosophy and should be maintained as much as humanly possible throughout our lives. We all need the help of other judoka and some good fortune to be really successful. Exhibit patience, tolerance, and understanding when other judoka propose novel ideas. Over time the productive ideas will be self-sustaining, and the other ideas simply will not work and fade away. The only time to speak quickly and firmly is when a new concept will threaten the safety of other judoka or is in opposition to the principles or the spirit of judo.

11) Remember where you came from and the people who helped you along the way. Your instructor(s) and your practice partners are the people who provided the path to your success. No one does it alone.

I remind myself often that judo is an activity designed for everyone, not just elite athletes or exceptionally strong people. Judo is about the proper execution of technique and using your opponent's strength and movement against him or her. Downplay the use of strength in practice while teaching proper movement and timing. Moreover, judo is about training your body and mind to be efficient and to deal with adversity in life successfully.

The following is a list of practice suggestions from the tenth dan Yoshitsugu Yamashita, President Theodore Roosevelt's instructor. They are as meaningful today as they were then. I keep them posted in the dojo where students cannot miss them.

Do's and Don'ts in Learning Judo

By Yoshitsugu (Yoshiaki) Yamashita
The First 10th Degree Black Belt

1) Study the correct way of applying the throws. Throwing with brute force is not the correct way of winning in JUDO. The most important point is to win with technique.

2) First learn offensive. You will see that defense is included in offensive. You will make no progress learning defense first.

3) Do not dislike falling. Learn the timing of the throw while you are being thrown.

4) Practice your throws by moving your body freely as possible in all directions. Do not lean to one side or get stiff. A great deal of repetition in a throw will be rewarded with a good throw.

5) Increase the number of practices and contests. You will never make any progress without accumulating a number of practices.

6) Do not select your opponents (which means do not say that you do or don't like to practice with a certain person). Everyone has his own specialty. You must try to learn all of them and make them your own.

7) Never neglect to improve the finer points. Practicing without any effort to improve will result in slow progress. Always recall your habits, as well as those of your opponent, while making improvement.

8) In practice put your heart and soul into it. It will interfere with your progress in practice if you keep on without this spirit.

9) Never forget what your instructor or higher ranking members teach you. During practice you will make great progress if you keep in mind what they have said to you.

10) Try to continue your practice as much as possible. Applying half-way will result in a very grave situation in your progress.

11) Watch and study throws as much as possible when trying to improve and advance. The technique and mind are just like the front and back of ones hand, meaning they are very closely related.

12) Refrain from overeating and drinking. Remember that overeating and drinking will bring an end to your practice and JUDO.

13) Always try to think of improvement, and don't think that you are too good. The latter is very easy to do while learning JUDO.

14) There is no end in learning JUDO.

Glossary of Judo Terms

A

ashi waza Foot or leg techniques

D

dan Grade (rank) holder (black belt)
dojo Judo practice hall

G

gatame Hold or lock
gari Reap
gokyo no waza Basic throwing techniques

I

ippon One point (in contest)

J

ju Gentleness or giving way
judo Gentle way; sport based on principles of jujutsu
judogi practice uniform
judoka Judo practitioner
jujutsu Art of combat techniques

K

kappo Resuscitation techniques
kata Form or shoulder
kodokan Institute of judo in Tokyo, Japan, founded by
  Dr. Kano
ko uchi gari minor inside reap
kuzushi breaking balance

M

mudansha Someone who holds a rank other than black belt

N

nage waza throwing techniques
ne waza grappling techniques

O

okuri eri jime sliding lapel choke
osoto gari major outer reaping (throw)
osaekomi immobilization, pinning
ouchi gari major inside reap

R

randori Free practice
rei Bow

S

sensei Teacher, instructor
shiai Contest
shido Note; small penalty
shime waza Strangulation techniques
shinpan Referee

T

tatame Practice mats
tori Person who does the throwing

U

uchikomi Repetitive form practice
uke Person who takes the falls
ukemi Break falls

W

waza Technique
wazari Half point

Y

yoko Side
yudansha: Black-belt holder
yudanshakai Association of black-belt holders

Bibliography and Further Reading

Adams, Neil. *The Neil Adams Guide to Better Judo.* London: Pan Books, 1988.

Ashida, Dr. Sachio. "Ethical Code and General Responsibility of Instructors." *USJF Handbook*, 1972.

Brousse, Michel, and Matsumoto, David. *Judo, a Sport and a Way of Life.* Seoul, Korea: International Judo Federation, 1999.

Campbell, Ben. *Championship Drill Training.* Sacramento, CA: Zenbei, 1974.

Cantanese, Anthony, J. *The Medical Care of the Judoka: A Guide for Athletes, Coaches, and Referees to Common Medical Problems in Judo.* Tucson, Arizona: Wheatmark, 2012.

Cunningham, Steven R. "Judo: Morality and the Physical Art." Presentation at the 1988 National Coaches Conference, OTC, Colorado Springs, Colorado, 1998.

Daigo, Toshiro. *Kodokan Judo Throwing Techniques.* Tokyo, Japan: Kodansha International, 2005.

Draeger, Donn F. *Modern Bujutsu and Budo.* New York: Weatherhill, 1974.

Fukuda, Keiko. *Born for the Mat, A Kodokan Kata Textbook for Women.* Kodokan, Japan, 1973.

Geesink, Anton. *My Championship Judo.* New York: Arco Publishing Company Inc., 1966.

Harrison, E. J. *The Fighting Spirit of Japan and Other Stories.* London: Foulsham, 1955.

Kano, Jigoro. *Judo (Jujutsu).* Tokyo: Buyu Shoseki Shuppan, 1937, 2001.

Kano, Jigoro. *Kodokan Judo.* Tokyo: Kodokan International, 1986.

Kodokan. *Illustrated Kodokan Judo.* Tokyo: Dai-Nippon Yubenkai Kodansha, 1955.

Mifune, Kyuzo. *The Canon of Judo, Classic Teachings on Principles and Techniques.* Tokyo: Kodansha International, 2004.

Nishioka, Hayward and West, James R. *The Judo Textbook in Practical Application.* Santa Clara, CA: Ohara Publications, Inc., 1979.

Ogasawara, Nagayasu. *Textbook of Judo.* New Jersey: Kokushi Dojo Inc., 1988.

Okano, Isao. *Vital Judo Grappling Techniques.* Japan: Japan Publications Inc., 1976.

Otaki, Tadao and Draeger, Donn. *Judo Formal Techniques, A Complete Guide to Kodokan Randori no Kata.* Rutland, VT: Charles E. Tuttle Company, 1983.

Otaki, Tadao and Draeger, Donn F. *Judo for Young Men.* Tokyo: Kodansha International LTD, 1965.

Sato, Nobuyuki and Inokuma, Isao. *Best Judo.* Tokyo: Kodansha International LTD, 1979.

Sato, Tetsuya and Okano, Isao. *Vital Judo.* Japan: Japan Publications Inc., 1973.

Yamashita, Yasuhiro. *The Fighting Spirit of Japan.* London: Ippon Books, 1993.

Watson, Brian N. *The Father of Judo, A Biography of Jigoro Kano.* Tokyo: Kodansha International, 2000.

About the Author

Mr. Roosa has been practicing judo for over forty-five years and is currently a member of Hudson Judo Yudanshakai, where he has attained the rank of godan. He is a member of their board of examiners and is promotion secretary. In addition, he has owned and operated Ulster Budokai Inc. in Kingston, New York, since 1976. He was formerly a National and North American Confederate Referee, now retired. In 2010 he was the recipient of the Ed Huyler Award from Liberty Bell Judo for his dedication to judo and in 2013 was honored with the Ralph Reyes Award for service as a judo referee. Mr. Roosa has also served as vice president of the Empire State Judo Yudanshakai, first treasurer of New York State Judo, and Hudson Valley judo chair for the New York State Empire State Games for over thirty years. As a referee he was a mat recorder in the first Women's World Judo Championships in 1980 and refereed national and international events for over twenty years, including the 1990 National Sports Festival and the US Open.

In addition to his judo credentials, Mr. Roosa holds a BS, MS, and CAS in education from SUNY–New Paltz. He is a retired physics, earth science, and math teacher, with over thirty years of experience at the elementary, middle school, and high school levels and has experience in educational administration.

CPSIA information can be obtained
at www.ICGtesting.com
Printed in the USA
LVHW05s1607260718
585000LV00003BB/13/P